As intimidating as this game looks, if approached properly, you can win the BIGGEST PRIZES IN THE PARK EASILY!! (Chapter 1)

This is one of the most popular games at amusement parks. Unfortunately, underhanded people have taken this game for a ride. IF YOU EVER CATCH SOME-BODY DOING THIS AT THIS PARTICULAR GAME, REPORT THEM TO THE PARK POLICE IMMEDIATELY!! (Ch. 4)

Why do they always have the sides roped off to the public in this particular game? If you ever have a chance to go around the corner on this game YOU WILL BE SHOCKED AT WHAT YOU SEE!! (Chapter 7)

Are you left-eye or right-eye dominant? Take this simple test to increase your chances of winning at this particular game TREMENDOUSLY!! (Ch. 2)

I DO NOT under any circumstances play these types of games at the fair. The state of Iowa has even forbidden some games to appear at their state fair!! (Chapter 12)

THE
SECRETS
OF
AMUSEMENT PARK GAMES
...REVEALED!

Brian Richardson
Silver Star Publishing

The Secrets of Amusement Park Games...Revealed!
2nd Edition
© 2002 by Brian Richardson
All rights reserved

ISBN 0-9669659-1-4

Silver Star Publishing
P.O. Box 6984
Houston, Texas 77265-6984

DISCLAIMER: This book is meant to entertain and offer only personal opinions by the author concerning how to approach certain amusement park, carnival, and fair games. Therefore, individuals still must play amusement park, carnival, and fair games at their own risk.

Table of Contents

Dedicated to all amusement park lovers
across the United States and the entire World.

Introduction

The title to this handbook, <u>The Secrets of Amusement Park Games...Revealed!</u> sounds rather provocative! After years of applying science, observation, **researched information**, and my own money, I have come up with a system that helps to increase an individual's odds of success at amusement park/state fair games around the country! (Pretty cool, huh!) During each year, there are an estimated 240 million people attending amusement parks throughout the United States. Untold millions will be attending local carnivals and big state fairs around the country from January to December. This also means that there will be lots of people playing carnival games who will donate millions of dollars to the amusement parks while trying to win the big stuffed animal! This doesn't even include income from food prices, soda pop, popcorn, souvenirs, ride passes, park entrance fees, parking charges, etc. It's a good thing water and oxygen are still free. (For now.)

Honestly, how many times have you actually won big time at these games? Once in a blue moon? Never? No problem! After you read this unique handbook, you can literally go to any amusement park in America and increase your chances of winning something!

I like understanding things. Did you know that magicians use fake legs to saw a woman in half? That Harry Houdini used a trapped door under a floor to "walk through a brick wall"? (For all you magicians out there, don't get too much heartburn. You can find this stuff at your local library with ease, or look at Fox Network's next magic special.)

Each chapter will give you clear and concise tips and pointers to maximize you chances of winning at these games.

Chapters 1 and 2 are my favorites of this whole system. Master these two sections and there's a good chance everytime you walk out of an amusement park you'll look like you have just raided a toy store!

Do you know why you can't get side access to this particular game at some city fairs? Why do they have this area roped off to the public? Read Chapter 7 to get the full inside story!

The last chapter, *Chapter 12- Games I Personally Avoid,* comes from years of research and observation in the games industry of amusement parks and carnivals.

I don't know about you, but I love the look on my son's face when I win a big stuffed teddy bear for him! I get a kick out of the looks of, "How did you win THAT?" on people's faces while stumbling down the midway with an oversized stuffed animal! (Or two! Or three!)

Within your lifetime, there's a good chance you will probably attend over 100 amusement parks, state fairs, and local fairs across the USA. It would be a great thing if you could win at these games over and over again!

Chapter 1- The Milkcan/Softball Toss

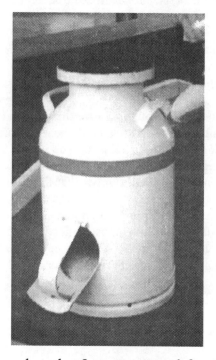

I vividly remember when I went to a now defunct amusement park on the east coast 18 years ago (Man, time flies like a B52). There was a host at the milkcan-softball toss coaxing people to spend $1 for 2 balls. "ONE IN AND YA WIN!" was his rallying cry. I walked up to this game and noticed huge stuffed animals dangling around the outside rafters of the booth. "Get outta here!" I thought. "That looks more impossible than me dunking a basketball like Dr. J!"

If I only knew then what I know now...

One of the mainstays of any state fair/ amusement park complex is this game. The concept is simple: one in and win. Due to inflation I doubt if you'll ever get the one-buck-for-two-balls deal again. (If you find a place that does, call me will ya?)

As intimidating as this game looks at first glance, its probably one of the easiest games to play! Unfortunately, many people don't see this game as simple at all. Next time you go to a state fair/ amusement park, check out the way they play. UGH!

The first type of player is the one who actually tries to throw the ball into the hole. The result is obvious.

DOINK!

The second type of person is a little better. He tries to make as soft an underhanded toss that he could make towards the hole. The result is not like the first, but it still doesn't go in.

CLANK!

Before I "spill the beans of my secret" on this game, lets look at some fundamental happenings which makes the secret to this game sooo successful.

If you could legally drop the ball a half a foot to a foot into the hole from directly above the canister, you shouldn't have any problem making the shot. (Unless you're more uncoordinated than Al Gore.)

Again, if you could toss the ball a half a foot away from the side, 99 out of 100 people would make it.

BRIAN! GET TO THE SECRET ALREADY!!!

OK. OK. No need to be pushy.

The secret is this: Toss the ball towards the canister BACKHANDED to create ample backwards spin on the softball.

Now let me go into detail about the secret, since I've gotten you to stop hyperventilating.

If you've ever played slow pitch softball, the first part of the secret seems logical and straight-forward. If not, use this example. While standing or sitting, visualize yourself with a softball in your throwing hand while trying to do the backstroke. Release the ball when your arm is in front of you.

The second part might need some clarification.

Remember the example I gave of dropping the ball from a foot directly over the canister? The greater the height you drop the ball from, the lesser chances you have of getting it in. When you keep the path relatively low (No McDonalds arch like shots PLEASE! You WILL lose!) you increase your chances of winning!

Where should you aim the ball?

The prime spot to aim the ball is the front lip. (The skill that it takes to do this requires only a small amount of fun practice, which will be covered later on.) The physics behind it goes as follows:

A top view of the milkcan.
Make sure to aim for the shaded area.

When the ball catches the front lip, the angle of the lip and the backspin cancel out a great deal of the energy that would make the ball bounce off the can. If you hit close to the center of the front lip, there's the added bonus of the ball possibly catching part of the hole, dissipating more energy of the toss and increasing the chances of the ball hanging around just long enough to trickle back into the hole. (Sir Isaac Newton would have been proud.)

Backspin kills the forward momentum on impact. Keeping the level of rise down kills the vertical (up & down) segment. The result should be a ball hitting the inside front lip area, fighting to get off a little, then finally dying some-where on the lip of the milkcan and trickling back into the hole. PLUNK! WE HAAAVE A WINNAH!! Remember, *you do not have to throw it directly into the hole to win*.

This is the only method I know that consistently allows a person greater chances to win. By doing the practice exercises, it has allowed me to almost walk into any state fair or amusement park in the country that has this game and come up a WINNER. The great part about it is that this game consistently offers the biggest prizes in the park. Giant dogs, big Tweety Birds, huge Sylvester the Cats -its all there waiting to be won!

Now, we all know the theory-looks-good-on-paper quote.
Here are some steps I need you to accomplish before going
to your local amusement park or state fair to conquer the
world. (At least it will feel like you are anyhow.)

A. Buy a softball from Wal-Mart or Kmart. They only
cost about a buck fifty. You can also find them at your
local sporting goods store for around the same price. If
you have a friend that plays league slow pitch softball,
swipe an old one from him.

B. Practice with a friend or by yourself. Usually,
having a friend works best, but working solo is no big
deal. Have your friend stand 8-10 feet away from you
while holding his hands cupped at nose level. (Of
course, have him extend his arms also. We don't want
to doink a good friend do we?) This crudely simulates
almost exactly the dimensions of the real thing. Use a
backhanded release, while simultaneously releasing
the ball at the level of his cupped hands. If you're by
yourself, practice in the basement or outside hanging a
bucket or something at nose level. Pace off 8-10 feet
and you're ready to practice! While we're at it, there
are two things that you should subconsciously keep in
mind while doing this:

B1. Relax. Hey, even though this is important to us,

its not a life and death matter either! Practice being real loosy-goosy while throwing. This also helps to facilitate a good wrist crank for the backhanded throw.

B2. Take your time. Unlike racing games, there's nobody to compete against. Use as much time as necessary, then let her fly!

Just to show how effective this system can be, I've tossed a sub-chapter in (Get it?) at no cost.

Chapter 1A - The Peach Basket Softball Toss

There is another variation of the softball throw game that involves peach baskets nailed to a wall at an angle. (Some places now have plastic baskets.) You've probably noticed this game the last time you were at a carnival or amusement park. Anyway, I remember being talked into spending my last dollars on this game as a kid -and losing badly. Didn't even come close. I walked around the park the rest of the day broke, dejected, and bummed out. (Don't you hear the 'sob story' violin playing in the background?) Fast forward 20 years.

The softball peach basket throw was around the corner. Visions of the past flooded my mind. I psychologically shied away from this game for a long time, but being curious if this system would work for this game as well as the milkcan softball throw, I decided to give it a whirl.

Admittedly the first couple of times I missed (due to rust) but I sensed that the system was actually working due to seeing how the ball responded to the basket. I gave it a confident system throw one last time. Clink! RATTLE, RATTLE, RATTLE! KERPLUNK! (It stayed in!!) WE HAVE A WINNAHH!

I must tell you this, I would rather play this game at an amusement park than a carnival or fair anyday. Here's why.

Usually at a fair or carnival, they coax you over by showing you how easy it is by tossing one in themselves. However, they are at a better angle and are closer to the basket than you are. " Its that easy," they tell you. So you play.

Let me digress from the story for a brief moment. The only place to aim at is close to the edge of the lip of the basket. Personally,I would only play peach baskets since they have less spring. Also if you are observant, you can see if the basket is worn or has a crack in it, which increases your chances of winning even more. There is a small margin of winning with the plastic bins but unless I'm in a carefree mood I don't chance them.

Anyway, if you miss, he will sometimes give you a free ball to practice with. If you are alert, on the free ball he will slip a ball into the basket. This usually makes the ball stay in the basket. If you are not alert to this, you will be greatly tempted to plunk down some more money to play again. (Ingenious some of these hosts are, huh?)

The next time I go to a carnival or fair, I'm going to ask them to toss the ball from where **I'm** standing. ☺

The greatest advantage of this system is that you do not have to be any type of athlete to do this. (If you have a pulse, you can play!)

These chapters arc two of my favorites of this whole system. Master this and there's a good chance you'll probably NEVER walk home from an amusement park, state fair, or carnival empty-handed.

Chapter 2 - The BB Gun Star Shootout

G 0003

All (Red) Star Must Be Shot From Card
To Win A Prize
This Target Void If Handled By Anyone Except Attendant

Any sharp shooters out there? Anybody out there who the only thing you've ever shot was the breeze? Have no fear. In fact, this game is quite fun to play -and to win at! This is another one of those games in which huge stuffed animals are doled out. Unfortunately, only one out of every 100 maybe actually win. This is strange, because next to the milkcan softball toss it's the easiest in the park to win big!

One of the main mistakes many players make is being fooled into thinking you need to obliterate every piece of red by shooting at the red only. I like to see the guys that come up to the game ala Rambo. RAT TAT TAT TAT TAT TAT!! It looks impressive but the objective is not achieved. Full of sound and fury signifying -nothing (Thanks ESPN!).

The secret to this game is kinda obvious:

Trace a shooting pattern _around_ the star and the star will fall by itself!

The HOW part is another matter, but very easy to learn. Stick with me and with a couple of practice tries you could be overloaded with stuffed animals. (That's if they're gracious enough to let you play again and again.) First, a little about the rifle.

If you're one of those souls who has never handled a weapon greater than a Super Soaker, let me assure you that unless you do something REAL stupid, you will not cause yourself or anybody else any harm. Also, there is very little, if any, recoil or kick-back from the rifle. It's safe to get up close and personal with it so you can actually aim through the sights. Sights are instruments on the rifle used to aim it in the right direction. They're very conspicuous on it, so you shouldn't have too much trouble finding it.

Now, here is the HOW part.

Let me start off by saying this: if you actually pick up a

rifle and hit what you're aiming for without any adjustments, you are:

A. A very good shot.

B. Lucky.

99.9% of the time the answer will be 'B'. All rifles have quirks and flaws that will make it shoot where you don't want to shoot. The good part of this info is that it will do this extremely consistently. So how do we hit what we want to hit?

Self-Zeroing comes to the rescue!

What is Self-Zeroing? It is a method used by the player to make adjustments to the built-in flaws of the weapon and use them to his advantage. What we are now going to do is walk through the process of playing this game from start to finish and tying in everything we've learned along the way. In this manner we will be able to get the full effect of the system.

First, lets start with posture. (Note that this part will be written with the shooting-illiterate in mind. If you know a thing or two about rifles, you can probably skip down a couple of notches.) I will be talking from a right-hander's point of view. All of you south-paws are backwards anyway. ☺

Make sure that your feet are flat on the ground. Grasp the rifle so that the butt rests somewhere supported on the right shoulder, your non-dominant hand cupping the rifle under the belly, your dominant hand on the handle with index finger light on the trigger, and your eye looking through the rear site towards the front site. (If you are right-handed this will be your right eye.) **Now here's the fun part**.

Aim right above the top of the point of the star, and rip off 3 BBs. Remember to lightly pull the trigger so as not to empty out too many. Where did the BBs hit? If they didn't hit above the star as aimed, DON'T WORRY! They should have at least hit the paper.

Draw an imaginary line from where you wanted the BBs to hit, towards where they did hit. The line hopefully isn't that long (about roughly half the length of the star is fine). We will call this line the crutch. We will call the place where you wanted the BBs to hit point W (for wanted to hit) and call the place where they did hit point D (for did hit).

Now we're going to take the "to hit here, aim there" approach. This calls for a dramatic flip in our thinking pattern. Now to hit that point above the star (which we want to treat as D1), draw the crutch line to a point W1 until its the same length and angle as the original crutch line. W1 is where you want to aim to hit D1!! (You're basically 'tricking the rifle' into hitting what you want to hit.) Try it. After a couple of tries at this game you'll be amazed. Rip off a couple of BBs.

Continue this system ripping around the star. About 3/4th of the way a significant amount of the star will be ripped out! Make sure you ration your bursts to 3-5 BBs a squeeze. Anything more will be wasting valuable ammo.

That's all there is to it. Around the second or third try (if you've never played this game before) you should be able to accomplish this with better than average consistency.

You'll be able to do some pretty amazing things. Recently, I was at a small city fair in which I was playing this game. All the red was gone, except for a little smidgen. "I see you got a tiny bit left there pardoner," said the host. "No problem," I replied, and proceeded to snip off the slither of red without blinking. The host was astonished. "You must be one of those Army boys, huh?"

Before I proceed to the next chapter, there are a couple of things I need to remind you of:

   A. Take a good stretch before playing. You will be bent over for a good 3-5 minutes. Warm up well so as not to strain something.

   B. Relax. Again, you're not racing against anybody. Take your sweet time. Leave the Rambo act to the guys walking away empty handed. If you are taking less than 2 minutes to complete this game, YOU ARE GOING TOO FAST!! Yes, you read that right. Take your time!

C. Try holding your breath <u>with all the air out of your body</u> while shooting. This will facilitate a steadier shot than just random squeezing. The process should go like this: inhale through pursed lips, exhale all the air out of your body via your nose, hold breath, aim, squeeze off a couple, inhale through pursed lips again. (Unless you don't appreciate oxygen.) Repeat. (Remember, inhale-pursed lips exhale-nose . Inhale-pursed lips exhale-nose.)

Why? Pretend that you're holding a rifle and aiming at something. (Make the object you're aiming at stationary, like a picture on the wall, an exit sign, etc. If it's a co-worker that's been getting on your nerves lately, tell him to stand still...) Inhale and exhale harder than normal. Did you see how your body (and more importantly your imaginary rifle) noticeably rose and fell? Even breathing normally will wreck havoc on your aim.

D. There has been some talk about this game being rigged due to the supposed bending of the barrels. I have YET to run into this problem. Remember, you're only 4 feet away from the target. If there are any discrepancies, self zeroing will take care of it.

E. You will probably see signs at this game that say something to the effect that the sights are in-accurate. USE THEM ANYHOW. Once again self zeroing comes to the rescue!

F. Remember this motto: "Hit the red, you are dead." Why? Besides wasting precious ammo, you will be doing double work. From my experience, in trying to trace around the star, you can only screw up a maximum of 2 times. The most frustrating thing that can happen to you is that you're almost there. You only need to shoot at a certain spot before the whole star collapses. You're licking your chops and all of a sudden -you squeeze the trigger. HIZZZ HIZZZZ. (You're out of ammo.)

Word of note. Are you left or right eye dominant? This determines whether you should be shooting left-handed or right-handed. Believe it or not, this can have a profound effect on even hitting SOMETHING. 90% of the time, if you're right handed, you're right eye dominant also. However, there is a small minority in the world that mother nature has played tricks on. Case in point:

I was at a bowling alley in Warren, Ohio in 1989 with some friends. We bowled two games. The first game I bowled a 52 (!). The second - 48. Needless to say, I was bummin'. (Especially due to the fact that there were two females there that cracked 100 with ease.) Determined not to let my self esteem digress, I diligently tried to answer to myself why I couldn't hit anything.

The next time we went out we bowled two more games. Nobody wanted me on their team. (Could you blame 'em?) First game 198. Second game 154. My friends were shocked. Some even thought that I "sandbagged" the first time. (Geez, give a fella deciding to use his brain cells some credit!)

What caused the dramatic change? I switched to bowling left handed. I'm not left-handed, but since my left eye is dominant, I could line things up easier. Jack Nicklaus, the famous pro golfer, has the same problem (Although he swings right-handed, watch how he first turns his head to his right to line his left eye up with the ball before he even starts to move the golf club.)

Which eye is your dominant eye? Take this test.

Pick out an object on a wall from where you are seated or standing. (A nail, small crack, lightswitch, or something small works best.) With both eyes wide open line your index finger up with that object. Holding that index finger position, close one eye while the other is still open. Switch eyes. Switch eyes. The eye in which the finger jumped off the object is your NON dominant eye.

The eye in which the finger STAYED on the object is

YOUR DOMINANT EYE.

Do this test.

From where you are seated or standing, with both eyes wide open, tilt your head until you see the ceiling. Hold that position and count *slowly* to ten. Do that now. Now read where the * is at the bottom of this page.

In short, determining what is your dominant eye, which determines what side to shoot from can make all the difference in the world.

Between this game and the softball toss its possible that you can win major stuff, as opposed to games where the best you can win is a rear-view mirror ornament. (Sort of like the difference between a Super-Sized McDonald's snack and a Happy Meal.) If you don't read any other chapters in this book, read this and the last chapter. The ratio between technique of winning and the size of the prizes is too good a deal to pass up. Happy shooting!

---

* Gotcha! Gotcha! (I know, that was juvenile. Here, I smack my own hand with a ruler for you. POW![YEOUCH!!])

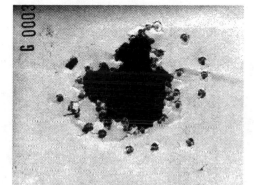

All (Red) Star Must Be Shot From Card
To Win A Prize

This Target Void If Handled By Anyone Except Attendant

WE HAVE A WINNER!!!

Chapter 3- The Ring Toss

The prizes given in this game are equal in size to the ones given in the milkcan/softball toss and the BB Gun Shoot. However, the level of difficulty significantly increases with this game. It's no wonder they give you a jumbo bowl of rings (about 50) for 3 bucks! Also, I have heard in some circles that the odds of winning this game are *600 to 1* or even more. Hey, give me <u>100 rings</u> for $3.00!

This is how the game is played. Over 300 2 litre bottles are arranged in a 15 by 20 rectangular pattern in the middle of a games shack. As stated above you're given a significant amount of hard plastic rings that are about 3 inches in diameter. Your objective is to 'ring' one of the 2 litre bottles around the bottleneck and you win.

Sounds simple huh?

A couple of years ago I played this game. Missing badly, I naturally asked the host for some pointers. "Throw the ring like a frisbee," he said. "I've seen a lot of people win with that technique."

I followed his advice and -used up my remaining rings. Needless to say, I took myself elsewhere. Cut to 1998.

At a famous amusement park on the east coast I tried this game again. I petitioned the host for some solid advice. "You know, out of 150 players that took part in this game yesterday only 15 won. The strange part is that the majority of the winners were children! I believe kids win more at this game because they 'will' it more."

Being of the analytical type, I dismissed the will part of his statement. However, the kid part stayed with me. Then it struck -KIDS ARE CLOSER TO THE LEVEL OF THE LITRE BOTTLES, THEREFORE THEIR RELEASE POINT IS CLOSER!! Their throwing arc is already relatively low. (Reread Chapter 1 if the significance of this point eludes you.)

Believe it or not, the first guy didn't give me bogus advice, but it only works if you frisbee throw from a level near the bottle tops. So, I shamelessly got on my knees to simulate the height of a kid. (Since I was in the position, I could petition for divine intervention. Maybe there is something in that "will it more".) I took dead aim at the center mass of all the bottles and flung one. CLICKETY CLICK CLICK DRIBBLE.

The ring action I got was incredible! Several times I nearly got one.

Once again, this is a very fun but very hard game to win at. However, I believe with the system of throwing the rings in a frisbee like manner coupled with a level-to-the-bottle top release you significantly increase your chances of winning! If they let you, stack 2, 3, or 4 rings together and throw them. This can increase your chances even more!

One popular method used by many adults is to find the closest bottle to them, hunch as far over as the host will allow, and try to 'lay' rings on the bottle. I deem this method utterly fruitless. Dropping the rings on the bottles cause too much force to ever successfully get one on. You must ricochet the rings to provide maximum chances of taking home the prize. Happy ringing!

Chapter 4 - The Golfball Roll Race Game

This is one of the most exciting games in the park! Let me tell you this. Its a <u>lot more fun</u> when you have 10 or more people participating. One time I played this game with only 3 people -with my wife and a total stranger being the other two! No fun. ☹ Also the prizes increase in size proportional to the number of people playing.

The object of the game goes as follows:

1. You're given a golf ball and you sit at the end of an

inclined table with colored holes or "chutes" at the top.

2. Usually the game is tied in with a theme. (Let's use racing horses since they are the most popular.) All the horses, including yours, are displayed on the back wall. You must beat everybody across the board to win.

3. The horse moves by rolling the golf ball into the chutes. The horse may move zero paces if it doesn't land in any hole except the one at the bottom, 1 pace for landing in a yellow chute, 2 paces for landing in a blue chute, and 3 paces for landing in the red chute. Obviously, the red chutes are furthest back.

4. You keep rolling your ball, taking it back from the automatic retriever, and roll it again until someone is declared the winner.

One of the very first things you can do is watch a couple of games and players to see if the game is acting properly. There have been accounts of people rolling the ball into the yellow chute and getting three hops. On the other side of that coin, some games have people just rolling it into the red chute -and have little if no progress. To be honest, only a small percentage (less than 1%) of these types of games have that problem.

At the beginning of the game, the host is usually cajoling and persuading people to participate. This gives you a golden opportunity not only to practice, but to find the shot for you that consistently gives good results. Types of shots that you can experiment with at that time are:

A. **The basic roll**. In a nutshell, you just simply roll the ball towards the chutes and hope for good results.

B. **The spin roll**. This type of delivery allows you to create "action" with the ball in order to achieve higher precision shots. Using a twisting motion with your thumb, index, and second fingers, you twist the ball while you do the basic roll. Variations of the spin roll include the left side spin, right side spin, and quarter turn spin.

C. **The bank roll**. In essence you bank the golfball off the side of the wall and let it ricochet back towards the colored markers.

D. **The bank spin roll**. This is the same as the bank roll but with a spin variation attached to it.

These are just the basics of many techniques used to <u>move your horse!</u> That's what the game boils down to doesn't it? If you have a special unorthodox technique you use (like rolling the ball while crossing your eyes) feel free to try it.

There are basically two important keys to winning this game. They are:

A. Rolling 2 and 3 hops. This is so self-explanatory, its almost like a person receiving 'a blinding flash of the obvious.' However, the second one eludes many people, and that is...

B. *Get the ball back as quickly as you can!* Your 3 hop is nowhere near as good as someone who rolls two 2 hops.

It's the most agonizing thing that can happen to you. You roll your ball, and it knocks around the chutes like a Ping-Pong ball -not dropping anytime soon. Finally, after crying and pleading and flat-out begging for the ball to drop somewhere, it falls down a chute. The worst case scenario is that you get zero hops -and the rest of the players are as far away from you as LA is from NY. How do we combat such a thing? It all goes back to the mini practice sessions that you take before the actual game. Make sure your shot consistently hits high hops and you quickly retrieve your ball.

Now, you have your special seat, you have your system down pat. You're ready to roll. (A lame attempt at a pun there...)

Now for some 'other' news...

A middle aged woman at a small carnival was playing this game with great success. She was beating everyone in sight, and had a Glad Bag full of stuffed animals and trinkets to prove it. She seemed obviously calm and pleasant. I was thinking to myself, "Can she really be that good, that lucky, that successful?" Unless she spent her life mastering this game like a chess player masters openings (which could be the case) something was fishy.

Cut to a major state fair south of the Mason Dixon line. As I was coming to the table, I noticed a guy walking away briskly. Obviously this individual didn't have that much common sense for as I looked down in his former ball hopper...I saw two balls.

Yes folks, the guy was doubling his chances.

The balls that they use at these games are regular range golf balls. Anybody can slip in with a ball and pretty much run the table.

I recommend two things:

> A.That the hosts of the game use colored golfballs that you see at miniature putt-putt games and change the colors everyday to avoid being taken.
> B. That if anybody recognizes a player that is doing this, the park police should be contacted to escort that

individual out of the park for an indefinite period of time. It's a great thing that most operators of these games know of this (especially at amusement parks) and have taken steps to prevent this.

To leave on a light note, I have a joke:

A guy goes to the doctor. Guy goes, " Doctor, my wife is driving me nuts!"

The Doctor says, " Oh, I see! It's nothing but stress. Here i: my simple perscription. Run 5 miles a day for thirty days and you should be fine!"

Thirty days pass, and the guy calls the Doctor.

> Doctor: " Ah, I see that you've done what I told you! How is your relationship with your wife?
> Guy: " I dunno, I'm 150 miles away from home…"

Chapter 5- Water Gun Race Games

This and the golf roll are the two most popular race games at amusement parks. Since park temperatures at many places hit the 90s during the summer months, just SEEING water is refreshing.

The object of the game is simple. On the command of the bell you squirt your water gun at a target (traditionally a clown's mouth) which starts pumping air into a balloon above the clown's head. Be the first to pop your balloon and you are the winner. Variations of this game include moving an object from start to a finish line before everyone else.

Once again, this is another one of those games that, to maximize your chances of winning, you must play more than once from the exact same spot. If you have read Chapter 2 you already understand that no two guns are alike. (Yes, squirt gun are included.) To clarify things, let me put the secret to this game up front and work backwards.

The secret is 95% getting the first jump on everybody by hitting the spot and 5% holding the position until you win.

Since everybody you're playing against is equally equipped with the same strength water gun, getting your balloon or marker moving is the difference between winning and losing.

Therefore, unless you're very lucky, or only playing against one other person (who happens to be Ray Charles), you're probably not going to win the first time. The time it takes to correct the initial water hosing to perfect aim (zeroing your gun -again!) somebody else probably is dead on accurate -and ahead of you.

On top of that, there might be (if ever so slight) variations in the balloons or markers. Even if your shot is straighter than six o'clock, that little fudge factor can tip the scales to

Joe Blow's favor. According to life probabilities, Joe Blow shouldn't win anything.

You're not Joe Blow.

So how do we combat all these things that are going against us to win? The first answer is straightforward:

> **A. Keep the same shooting posture for both games**. You have to apply some memory skill to this tip. Were your elbows together or apart? Were you hunched over the rail or were you sitting straight up? This is important stuff, because it flows right into 'B'.

> **B. Make sure, the first time you play, that you recognize where the water initially hits before you correct your aim**. If you don't win, that information will be very valuable to you the next time! Use this data to make the artificial zero adjustment we talked about in Chapter 2. Once that adjustment is made, you will more than likely get the jump on everybody else. This is what we want!

Follow these tips, and your chances of winning should increase dramatically!

Chapter 6 - The Curly Bar Ring Guide

This is one of the newer games at amusement parks across America. The object of the game is to guide a circular shaped washer around a curly bar all the way to the base of the game. This is one of the most demanding yet rewarding games in the park! The stuffed animal prizes for a person who conquers this game are enormous. (Big enough that you probably have to pay an extra admission ticket for it. (Just kiddin'!) It calls for a steady hand, nerves of steel, and friends not throwing off your concentration.

The object of this game is simple. A sensitive curly wire (that's revolving counter-clockwise) is before you. You're given an instrument that looks some thing like:

$$==O==$$

Your mission is to grasp the handles of this instrument and navigate the O (washer) onto the curly wire all the way to the base. There's one catch -you cannot touch the wire with the inside of the O. If you're not successful, a red light with a buzzer comes on that lets you and everyone within 100 feet of you know that you've failed. If you're successful, you will get a happily flashing red light, and maybe some applause.

One of the things I noticed by playing this game and watching it myself is that at least 10 out of 10 guys and girls get half-way down the bar. Blind people included.

Now here's what happens...

The player:

> **A. Starts getting nervous**. His palms are sweating like a pig. (Do pigs actually sweat?) Crowds start gathering around anticipating your victorious run down the bar. Your wife/girlfriend can feel the giant

stuffed animal manifest itself in her arms as you continue. "Good grief! Back up people!" you mumble to yourself. The pressure is just too intense. ZAP! AWWWW...

B. Starts getting careless. You're not nervous. As a matter of fact, you're doing pretty good. No shakes here. On your way to winning, a stray thought enters your mind for a split second. ZAP! "Fiddlesticks!"

C. Starts getting overconfident. You're doing okay. Your buddy vultures swarm in sensing the kill. He starts thinking to himself, "C'mon John! You're winning. Halfway there!. Hey, I'm doing good. Oh boy, my girlfriend is gonna love this stuffed animal. Almost home, baby! John,you are the MA...ZAAAP!" 'AWWWW!!" he yells. 'I WAS THIIISS CLOSE'... Unfortunately, as that hackneyed saying goes -close only counts in horseshoes.

D. Catches a cramp. No kidding. You're pretty much bent over at the waist for the whole game. Some people just go for it and they literally get zapped before the game gets them. ARRRGHH! ZAP!

PSSST!! Did you know that you can tell if a person has a good chance of winning or losing just by the way he or she starts? Its true. Believe it or not, there are only two ways to put the washer around the beginning of the curly bar to

44

start the game. One will give you good chances; the other will give you troubles.

Ask any host for a demonstration at this game and they will start off right. By the way most host of this game are pretty good at it since they have the time to practice it.

Grab a pen or pencil and hold it with both hands at both ends. Now remember that the curly bar rotates counter clockwise.

If you put the washer on the tip of the curly bar and your hands are moving **away** from your body, kiss a good portion of your chances of winning goodbye. As a reference, the tip will be around the 4, 3, or 2 'o clock position when you do this.

If you put the washer on and your hands are moving **towards** your body, you're on the right track. As a reference, the tip of the curly bar will be around the 10, 9, or 8 'o clock position.

Why is this? It has a lot to do with the position that you're in once you are half-way down the bar. One will put you in far better position to complete the final half than the other.

Assuming that you are on the right track, the last part requires a lot of concentration. You have the bar flattening out near the bottom while the whole curly bar is rotating at

45

a pretty brisk rate. How do we get to the bottom to get that happy flashing light?

Have you ever done maze puzzles before? A lot of people know that the best way to solve them is to do them backwards from the finish to the start. Before you play this game, visualize the ring already at the bottom and work your way back to about the middle. This will give you a good feel as to where you need to turn the washer and what position it needs to be in.

The horizontal part at the bottom of the ring that leads to the end should be travelling from the 11 to 7:30 position when you make your move.

So as to not overload you with a mind full of keys, there is one body position that you must have in order to succeed at this game. Let's start with a made up term called the kruck. The kruck is the 1 inch area in which the bar just starts to flatten out leading to the horizontal section leading to the goal. This is the area in which you need to concentrate on when the horizontal section is travelling between that 11 and 7:30 position. If you have just made it or are travelling to that area just before the kruck AND the horizontal bar is travelling in that 11-7:30 moving zone, *your body position changes*.

Diagram showing man on left in starting (and playing) position and same man on right before the 'kruck' and horizontal bar in 11-7:30 zone. Body twisted to left. Left leg straight. Right leg bent in.

Once you hit that area, your body tilts and twists to the left. Your body position should not be directly in front of the game as if you just started, but to the right edge of the game. Why? When you are in this position, it gives you that extra split second needed to whip the washer around the kruck, across the horizontal bar, and land in beep-beep-beep land. The window of opportunity is tight, so you have to be absolutely mentally ready.

Phew! Let me say that you can follow what I'm saying a lot easier if you had this game directly in front of you. Let me also say that this is not the only method of winning at this game. I do feel that my method had a fundamental soundness to it.

Some final thoughts:

1. If you're not a naturally cool headed and steady handed person, go play something else. (Or just laugh at your buddies as they get zapped repeatedly.)

2. If your hand shakes more than a washing machine and you're less cool headed than General Custer and STILL want to play, here are a few tips:

  a. Take a good stretch before you start. Its bad enough that you want to play. We don't need a cramp to factor into the situation. ☺

  b. Try to block out everything around you and focus on your washer and the bar.

  c. Don't forget about the 'kruck' and the flattening out part of the bar.

2. This is for Joe Cool. DO NOT GET EXCITED OR OVERCONFIDENT IN IN ANY WAY, SHAPE, OR FORM. You might have to apply some reverse psychology here but its well worth it.

Chapter 7- The Basketball Shoot

There are scientific studies that show that the closer the release point is to basketball rim level, the more likely your shot will go in. No wonder they put those rims 11 to 12 feet in the air at amusement parks and carnivals!

However, this does not mean that your participation in this game is a lost cause.

I have one recommendation for everybody. Boy, girl, man, and woman. Age 8-80. That's if you want to increase your chances of winning. **Shoot underhanded.**

I can hear a couple of guys reading this snickering uncontrollably. "What?? Lose all my 'cool points' that I've amassed over the years???" you ask incredulously. Hey, look at Rick Barry, the former NBA great who has the highest free throw percentage in NBA history. I could perceive a lot of guys yukking it up when he did it. (Rick Barry is in the Basketball Hall of Fame. Take that.)

Seriously, one of the main reasons for this suggestion is that I feel that the balls used for these games are modified in some way. They look like real basketballs but they just don't have the same feel. Some are over inflated. Others feel like bricks for some reason.

For some reason, some hosts will not let you shoot under handed. At a large fair in the south, I was about to assume the position. "Mac, you can't do that."

"I can't shoot underhanded?" I asked.

"Nope. Gotta be a man about it. No granny shots."

I was about to give him the Rick Barry speech, but gave the guy some grace. He did say that the reason he didn't allow 'granny shots' is because they give the player an almost perfect arc and angle for winning. Another reason why he didn't allow it may be due to the next story.

A couple of years ago I attended a small town fair that had the 12 foot high rim. The rules again were 1 in and win. Being an observant type I noticed others who were playing and throwing up clankers. The funny thing was that a couple of athletic looking guys were clanking it also. Repeatedly.

I don't know what got into me, but I thought the direct opposite of , "Man, if these guys are heaving bricks, I don't need to be playing!" I gave the lady my two bucks.

BOINK! CLANK!! I gave the lady two more dollars.

This time I got off a good shot. I knew it was all net, until it rumbled on the rim and dribbled off. Embarrassing. (NOTE: At that time I was still shooting overhanded.)

I saved the rest of my dollars for something else. Just curious, I walked around to the side of the game and OHHHHHH! Aha...

Somebody noticeably took a sledgehammer to the rims making them ovals instead of round. From the front though they look completely normal, thanks to the height and the shadows surrounding the rim. During the day it is equally difficult to detect.

Is this legal? Believe it or not the answer is yes. During the last couple of years many of these games have put up a sign in clear view that says something to the effect: 'Not Regulation Rims'. Games can be altered by the company to make it harder but not impossible to win. Is it unfair? Not really, but again this was not meant to be regulation basketball goal. Note that <u>I have never seen this done at a major amusement park.</u>

For the initiated (those who have shot a basketball before), still keep in mind these points:

A. Relax completely. Nothing in the world ruins a good shot more than being tense.

B. Use your legs and glutes to power the shot. Its a long ways up. You need all the power you can get.

C. Play twice to "zero" your shot and increase chances of winning. In essence, you know where you went wrong the first time. Make intelligent adjustments and shoot accordingly.

A final note. When you go to the amusement park this year, analyze this game. People treat it like foul shooting when you're actually a lot farther back. This makes the argument for shooting Rick Barry style all the more powerful. Some parks even dole out stuffed animals similar in size to the milkcan softball toss!

One basketball game at the amusement parks I usually stay

away from is the one foot diameter rim basketball toss.
You've probably seen it before. In my opinion, hardly any
chance of winning and more importantly, the prizes are not
proportional to the level of difficulty. It is a fun game for
kids –provided that they give you a prize whether you win
or lose. (I have seen some places use this policy. I think its
great! Even though the no-win prize is smaller, at least the
person walked away pretty happy.)

Chapter 8- The Age/Weight Guess

These guys are good. Especially at weight guess games.

Unless you're wearing a hefty bag to hide your body frame, its pretty difficult to cover up those tell-tale signs of how much you weigh. They will look at a lot of things: stomach, thighs, buttocks, body frame, cheek bones, etc. Don't be amazed if he even hits "the proverbial nail on the head" with an exact answer. With a little practice, you could do the same thing. (But with 1/3 of the American population being overweight that would be kinda depressing, wouldn't it?)

The point I'm trying to make is unless you have body

features that are unusual and atypical that hide or give the illusion of weight, you will get nailed 9 times out of 10. Play the age guess game? It offers you slightly greater winning chances, but once again these guys are good. If you're in your 30's you can start right now smoking 3 packs of unfiltered cigarettes a day and drink 90 proof liquor so that in a years time NOBODY could guess how old you really are. What a price to win a game that at best doles out glass mugs with the amusement park logo on it.

Once again, these people have a pretty fair idea of how a typical 40 year old male should look like and several give-aways on the human anatomy to confirm it.

The next time you go to an amusement park, watch the host of this game closely. He or she is very observant. While he talks his eyes are roving all over the participants. Part of his brain is crunching and voila! He spits out a pretty accurate figure. Impressive.

Two people they couldn't guess the age on are my wife and my mother. My wife looks 15 years younger than her age. My mother?

My mom and I went on a trip to a museum in the south when I was about to graduate from college. As the tour guide was taking us around, she asked me nonchalantly,

"Is your wife from this area?" nodding towards you-know -

who.

I steamed, " THAT'S NOT MY WIFE!! THAT'S MY MOTHER (YOU IDIOT)!!!" Of course, Mom was flattered...

This is one of those games that you just play for laughs and to enjoy the park experience. You should only consider this a pleasant diversion. Anything beyond that is a lost cause.

Chapter 9- The Baseball/Football Throw

These games are strictly for athletes. I almost killed a host of a game with a 60mph fastball to nowhere in particular. The poor guy had a look on his face that said, " Can't you just go to the Ring Toss Game, huh pal?"

The prizes are not giant sized in many of these games, but its a good way to show off to your friends, wife, or kids (although a BETTER way to show off would be to re-read one of the previous chapters and go win a big one!). Many of the variations in this game are as follows:

A. The Clown Dunk: Ah yes. This game has been around forever. Usually you get three balls for a buck to hit a circular dot about 1 foot in diameter to dunk a clown who is busy insulting your manhood and talking about your mom. Once again, if you're not good at throwing stuff, don't risk it. These clowns can bring grown men to tears with their put-downs (HEY FOLKS, LOOK AT EINSTEIN OVER HERE TRYING TO DUNK ME!! GUY'S SO STUPID I SAW HIM IN A 99 CENT STORE ASKING FOR A PRICE CHECK…)

B. The Football Toss: This game is pretty basic. You have to throw a certain number of footballs through tires or marked partitions to win.

C. The Three Bottle Knock Off: This game is an old stand by also. The object is to knock all three bottles (which seem like they're full of lead) completely off the platform to win. Even people who I thought were going to win just knocked them down but not completely off. I asked a host one time where's the best place to aim for this game. He told me below center mass between the two bottom bottles. Anywhere else will lead to futility. [This reminds me of a situation in which, unfortunately, a tornado hit a popular small amusement park on the east coast. The place was absolutely leveled. Total devastation. Only thing still standing was those three milk bottles...] Just a tip for the athlete. Did I tell you I almost beaned a guy?

D. The Three Cat Knock Down: This game is also a mainstay at amusement parks. About 15 rows of 20 cats align a wall. Your job is to knock over 3 consecutive cats and you win. Believe it or not, this game just might afford the novice a chance to win, since there are so many cats up there. Even stray shots might just hit something. The funny part is that those cats have a LOT of fur around them. You must hit the cat squarely, or not at all.

In a nutshell, if you don't have a good throwing arm, like t take abuse, and are as about athletic as a Basset Hound-go right ahead. Forewarned is forearmed.

Chapter 10- The Golf Putting Game

To cater to the growing number of Tiger Woods wannabes, this game appeared on the scene - with a little amusement park tweaking of course!

Some parks have different variations on this game. One park has you to putt from about 10 to 15 feet with big holes for kids and make-shift sand traps in the middle of the game. Another park has you putting so far away from the hole you're in another zip code.

If the only club you've ever held in your life is of the soda variety, you might need a few pointers.

A. Observe a few players do it before you. This should at least get you to first base as far as understanding what you need to do. Doesn't look that hard, huh?

B. When holding the club, take out all the wildcards in your stroke. This means that anything that could detract from hitting the ball squarely should be eliminated. The most common culprits are:

B1. The Arms. If you observe some players, their arms are going every which way but straight. The best way to keep the arms in alignment with your stroke is to weld your elbows and upper arms to the sides of your body.

B2. The Legs and Feet. It all boils down to alignment. You're never going to sink anything if you're not pointed in the right direction. The traditional way is to stand with your feet perpendicular to the path the ball is going to travel.

B3. The Hands. I recommend that you grip the club with your fingers instead of any palm handling. This will ensure greater control over the putter.

C. Take a few phantom practice strokes to ensure everything's OK before the real thing. Once again, this is not a race game. Relax and take your time before you're ready.

It is advisable that you play this game maybe two to three times to ensure maximum chances of winning. Why is that? Well, remember at the top I told you that amusement parks give their own twist to these games? Its true, although it's not anything a seasoned golfer wouldn't know about.

In the majority of these games I've seen, there is a green carpet placed over plywood. Depending upon the weather and other factors, both can have a significant effect upon the way the ball travels toward the hole. Therefore, use the first try as an indicator of the 'break' on the carpet, then plan your second ball accordingly.

At a famous amusement park in Virginia, I had the chance to put this system to the test. I aligned my putt for a shot straight at the hole. It broke to the right about a half-foot before it reached the hole. On the next ball, I took this new data into account and aimed a good foot to the left of the hole. I think I looked kinda silly to some onlookers as I probably heard some snickers. Undaunted, I took my aim and gave it a nice, gentle, and controlled putting stroke. The ball seemed like it had no chance until little by little the ball started breaking right...into the cup! KERPLUNK!! WE HAVA WINNAHH!!!

I turned around and saw looks of astonishment on two particular stranger's faces. I smiled, received a large stuffed dog, and gave it to my wife. (She was quite pleased.)

I think I'm ready for the PGA Tour. ☺

Chapter 11 - The Sign-Ball Bounce Off Game

I walk up to this game at a carnival on the east coast. The host starts his banter. " Step right up, son! Win a stuffed animal for your lady! One in and ya win." He gives a brief demonstration. Taking a whiffle ball in his hands, he gently tosses it towards the tilted sign.

Dink. It hits the sign. Plop. It falls feather-like into the basket below.

" Is that all there is to it? " I ask.

"That's all there is! Why, even Stevie Wonder could play this game and win!!"

I give the host two bucks for one ball. CLANK. The ball crashes into the sign. BONK. The ball hits the ground three feet in front of the basket.

" Look fella. This is the easiest game in the park. Pay attention now." Dink. Plop.

My turn.

CLANK. BONK.

A toddler waddles up next to me. " Googoo gaga zssrppt!" (That's baby talk for, "You're throwing it too hard! Watch me.") With a milk bottle in one hand and a ball in the other, he makes a toss.

Dink. Plop.

By this time, steam is coming out of my ears. " Give me three more balls!" I demand.

CLANK. BONK. CLANK. BONK. ("Come on, Brian! Concentrate!!") CLANK. BONK.

A Labrador retriever comes by and notices my troubles.

"Arf! Ruff! Bow Wow!" (Translation: "No.No. No. You must do it like this!") The dog paws a ball.

Dink. Plop.

ARRRRRGGGGGGHHHHHH!!!!!

I wake up in a cold sweat. My wife is beside me -sound asleep.

This is one of _the_ most ingenious games ever made for a fair or amusement park! It just LOOKS SO DARN EASY. To add insult to wallet injury, the game host seems to make 4-5 in a row with ease. How does he or she do it?

Usually this game costs $2 for one ball and 3 balls for $5. The object of the game is to bounce a whiffle-ball off a sign bent at about a 45 degree angle so that it falls into a rectangular basket placed below the sign.

After spending a considerable amount of money on this game, I stumbled onto the secret by accident. I was throwing a ball that felt like it slipped out of my hand. I thought I wasted a shot, until it hit the sign. Dink. Plop. I was shocked. "We hava winnah!!" barked the host. I remember just standing there wondering how I could duplicate the feat. After giving it some thought, the light bulb went on. I smiled so hard, I almost pushed my ears to the back of my head.

My observations are threefold:

   a. When you release the ball from your hand, release
   it so that it does not spin directly forward, but a little
   bit to the right or left. This helps dissipate the energy
   of the shot, thereby increasing its chances of falling
   into the basket.

   b. Make sure you hit the sign in the area between the
   middle and the top foul line.

   c. You think not so much of hitting the sign, but
   rather putting ample spin on the ball so that it hits the
   sign as dead as possible! (Watch the host the next
   time you see this game. They let the ball do the work!)

Another thing you must know. The host are not doing
anything that you can't do yourself in this game. A lot of
them have the time to practice this. Personally, I feel if
anybody had a chance to practice this game non-stop for a
small period of time, they would nail it consistently also.

In order to increase your chances of winning this game to
the maximum, do the following:

   A. Go by a set of cheap whiffle balls at a dollar store.
   Usually they come in a three for a dollar pack.

B.Buy a piece of wood or get something around the house to simulate the sign. Make sure its at chest level. (You may have to set it on a chair or table.) Pace off approximately 4 feet from the board.

1.Begin to simulate the exact motions needed (as stated above) in order for the ball to drop into the basket. In this case, imagine a basket right below the sign.

2. Make sure that your arm is fully extended.

Again, this is one of those games that you really need to practice on a home made set up before being able to win at this consistently. Many times you see what are called 'oopsies'. The person is concentrating so hard that when they throw it, the ball clanks into the board or flies right over the whole sign altogether! Knowing the how behind this game is good, but practicing to prevent those 'oopsies' (like in the milkcan softball toss) go a long way.

Chapter 12- Games I Personally Avoid!

Millions of people will be coming to amusement parks and state fairs across the USA to have a good time with their families, friends, and loved ones. The last thing on their minds is having somebody take them for their money without a fair and square shot at winning.

If you've already read the preceding chapters you know about the sledgehammered basketball rims and the lead-like bottles in the baseball throw. As I said before, these types of games still give the player a measurable chance of winning. The greater majority of major amusement parks do not have these types of games, only games of skill. So you can be assured that most amusement park games, however difficult they seem, are winnable.

These are the games that I would stay away from:

A. **Any Game in which the outcome is literally in the hands of the host**. Some of these games include the ones that say whether you win a small, medium or large prize. (Or nothing at all!) Some are addition operations in which you have to get a certain number to win. (Here's a good one. If the rules are so confusing that a rocket scientist would have trouble understanding it, move on!) I have yet to see anyone win big at these types of games. At a local fair in

Baltimore, Maryland I once witnessed a guy lose over $200 at these games with the promise by the host that, " You're getting warmer, Doc!" The only thing getting warm was the host's pockets. There have been incidents in the past where out of 100 items, floating ducks, cups to knock down with S,M, or L (small medium or large) written on it only one or two are Ls. And some don't have any! The point is **you** don't know. Believe it or not, the state of Iowa has regulations written in their code to prevent some of these games from showing up at the Iowa State Fair! The only games that I would do a 180 turn on are the duck and fishing games –provided that I have a kid with me. (Since I won't play those myself.) It's a fun thing for them to do. Otherwise, I avoid these games.

B. Test of Strength - Game. " Step right up! Step right up! Test your strength! Ring the bell 3 times and win a doll for the lady!" This game is so old, Moses probably played it. This game caters to the macho guy who thinks he can knock the bell off its hinges. Usually the device has markers from 'momma's boy' to 'Hercules' to 'wimp' written on the pole. Too bad he doesn't know that this game can easily be tweaked to make sure you don't have any ice cube's chance on the equator of winning. Next time you go to the local fair, observe these things

B1. There is a wire supporting the sliding weight. It

runs from the bottom of the pole to the bell, then passes through a loop or pulley to become one of the guy wires supporting the pole.

B2. Secret time: It is impossible for the marker to make it up the pole on a slack wire. The host leans against the wire to make it taut, then steps away to make it slack. In a nutshell, the host has complete control over who wins, who doesn't, who to tease with 2 rings and leave 'em dry on the third attempt, etc.

There you have it, folks! You're now more educated about these things than most of the general public.

A Final Note…

If you find yourself not winning at any games in the park, or any particular game, no matter how much the hosts badger you…

…Walk away.

Yep. You read that right. (Remember rent? Car notes? Mortgage? Groceries??) It might be a case in which you need to practice more. The best thing you can do is have a predetermined budget of how much you will allow yourself to spend on games, souvenirs, food, etc. *and stick with it!!* When I see an ATM inside an amusement park, and the urge to spend more than I need hits, I visually see it exploding.

If you are with a date and happen not to be doing so well, see if you can set up a two race competition on one of the two race games mentioned during a slow period for the host. If you are a guy and you win, you give her the stuffed animal. If she wins –she keeps it! (Talk about a win-win 'no lose'- 'no lose' situation!) You can also buy her something from the gift shop.

Appendix A
Richardson's 'Official' Top 10
Wooden and Steel Roller Coasters in America!

You start up a steep hill knowing you can't stop what is about to happen. An anxiety induced knot forms in your stomach as you taste a saltiness in your mouth. You feel an imaginary sweat form on your forehead as you hear the train make its eerie climb. "Claka, claka, claka, claka,..."

The smell of fresh air mixed with a faint scent of oil engulfs the atmosphere. The earth looks smaller and the people on the ground look like ants as you rise towards the clouds. Whatever you were holding on to or touching is grasped a little tighter, as if the mere act of grabbing something will save you from your upcoming fate.

You're almost at the top. Calling for Mommy won't help you. Crying is of no use. Prayer is futile.

You try to catch one final breath.

Too late.

WHOOOOOOOOOOOOOSSSSSSSSSHHHHHHHHHHHH!!!!

"YAAAAAAAAAAAAAAAAAAAAAAAAAAAAHHHHHIIH..."

Roller coasters and amusement parks have been an integral part of the American landscape. During the 1920s, there were over 1,400 rollercoasters across the United States. Some of these jewels are still standing and are giving new generations of Americans the same thrills given to their parents and grandparents! Today, we are in a roller coaster renaissance!! New ideas combined with the advent of powerful computers allow designers to make safer, stronger, and scarier rides for all to enjoy!

All roller coasters were judged by these criteria: first drop, speed, air-time (This is when your backside leaves the seat and the top of your thighs hit the lap bar for a second or two.) and the all-important terror factor.

These are my humble opinions. Therefore, if you don't see your favorite roller coaster on this list, it doesn't mean that it is a dud.

Now buckle up. Keep all hands, arms, and other body parts inside the train at all times. Passengers are reminded to make silly or crazy faces towards the camera taking your picture. Sit back. Relax. (If you can.) Enjoy the ride!

The Top 10 Wooden Roller Coasters in America!
(In descending order.)

10. Comet - HersheyPark
HersheyPark, PA

This is more of a sentimental pick than anything. The first drop is just so-so. Airtime is OK. It has the terror factor of a miniature daschsund. (I own one. The worst they will do to you is lick you to death.) However, there is a certain beauty to it that I just don't experience from any other coaster. There are no quantitative explanations. I JUST LOVE IT. Enough said.

9. Grizzly - Paramount Kings Dominion
Doswell, VA

Another one of those unimpressive-first-drop-but-WATCH-OUT rollercoasters! The dive into a very dis-orienting tunnel marks the beginning of great speed and airtime! The setting in the woods adds to the visual effect. They have cut out a significant part of the woods to make room for another coaster recently. Tight curves and speed bumps are the rule as you head back towards the station.

8. Texas Giant - Six Flags Over Texas
Arlington, TX

Since its debut in 1990, the Texas Giant has received much praise and continues to do so to this day! From the first drop all the way to the station, this coaster runs like tap water! With a 137 foot drop at a steep 53 degrees, the Texas Giant reaches speeds up to 67 mph! The best part is the disorienting chase back to the station!

7. Legend – Holiday World
Santa Claus, IN

This gem of a coaster opened to rave reviews on May 6, 2000! This Custom Coasters International made beauty has all the characteristics of an outstanding coaster. Suspense, decent first drop, airtime, and big time surprises makes this a must ride for any coaster enthusiast!

6. Phoenix - Knoebels Amusement Resort
Elysburg, PA

All I have to say is... thank God for lap bars! Built in 1947, this coaster first appeared as the Rocket at the now defunct Playland Park in San Antonio, TX. It was moved to Knoebels in 1985, to the delight of many! The first drop is fine, but the airtime is so severe, you feel as if you'll wind up near the Merry-Go-Round! (By the way, they have the best bumper cars also.) I envy anybody who has ridden this great coaster at night!

5. Raven - Holiday World
Santa Claus, IN

Wow! This coaster has some giddy-up! I had the pleasure
to ride it after a rainfall too! (A little moisture on the track
usually amounts to more speed.) The one that gets you is
the drop in the middle of the run! Although the ride lasts
only a short one minute and forty seconds, all the plusses
more than outweigh the brief ride. Two Top 10 Roller
Coasters in one park! Way to go!!

4. Georgia Cyclone - Six Flags Over Georgia
Austell, GA

Without a doubt one of the most terrifying roller coaster in
America! Especially if you ride it for the first time! This
coaster is twice as mean as its daddy up in New York.
Once again, looks can be deceiving. Sit near the back and if
the first drop doesn't scare ya, you must be in a coma!
Amazing disorientation, massive airtime, and flat out break
neck speed makes this roller coaster another one of my sentimental favorites to ride!! (There are some delightfully
frightening secrets about this ride that I just can't talk
about, for fear of ruining your trip!) Ride at night for
maximum impact!

3. Shivering Timbers - Michigan's Adventure
Muskegon, MI

If there was a 1998 Rollercoaster Rookie of the Year
award, this gorgeous woodie would have won hands down!
With a vertical drop of 120 feet at a steep 53.25 degrees,
this Custom Coasters International gem makes your
stomach disappear, gives you good airtime, and scares the
heck out of you! I love it when the designers use optical
illusions to heighten ride intensity! (No secrets on this one
either! Go and ride it!)

2. Boss – Six Flags St. Louis
Eureka, MO

Without question, one of the most significant coasters in
America is located in the 'Show-Me' state! (This coaster
will show you something –that's for sure!!) Amazing air
time and intensity ending with one of the most spectacular
helix runs of any coaster on the planet will literally take
your breath away!

1. Ghost Rider – Knott's Berry Farm
Buena Park, CA

Rising 118 feet above the park, this state-of-the-art-
wooden roller coaster has thrilled (and *terrified*) all who
have ridden it! The ride starts with an initial 108 foot drop

(that's **banked**) at an angle of 51 degrees!! From there, THE RIDE JUST TAKES OFF!!! Massive airtime, breakneck speed, and sheer intensity are its hallmarks! A unique feature of this ride is that it actually gives you a break during the halfway point –just to catch your breath and take a look around, before it JUST GOES ON A MAD RUSH AGAIN!! Simply the most amazing Wooden roller coaster in America!

The Top 10 Steel Roller Coasters in America!
(In descending order.)

10. Big Bad Wolf - Busch Gardens Williamsburg
Williamsburg, VA

The first of its kind, the Big Bad Wolf continues to be standard suspended roller coaster by which others are measured! Reaching speeds upward to 50 mph as you wind through a remodeled Bavarian Village, the ride culminates with a heart-stopping 100 foot plunge towards the Rhine River! Worth the price of admission alone! If it wasn't for that airbrake at the top of the hill, I think I would have passed out!

9. Batman the Ride
Six Flags Over Georgia (Austell, GA) Six Flags Great America (Gurnee,IL)
Six Flags Magic Mountain (Valencia, CA)
Six Flags St. Louis (Eureka, MO) Six Flags Over Texas (Arlington, TX)
Six Flags Great Adventure (Jackson, NJ)

The first time I rode this, I needed 3 minutes to get my bearings back! For sheer intensity and tightness of the ride it *kicks*! It seems as if it picks up more and more speed until you're back in the loading dock. Note that these are "cookie cutter coasters" that Six Flags has put in the majority of their parks that were built by Bolliger & Mabillard of Switzerland. A high quality roller coaster at 6 locations! Excellent ride!

8. Chang - Six Flags Kentucky Kingdom
Louisville, KY

This roller coaster is so big, you can see it from Interstate 65! Ride in the front to catch the view; ride in the back to catch all the Gs! The turns near the end are impossibly tight! (I wonder how much loose change the park custodians find down there at the end of the day!) Excellent ride!

7. Alpengeist -Busch Gardens Williamsburg
Williamsburg, VA

I can hear the howling as some people read this! "What? This isn't even #2??" you cry. Visually, its beautiful. (Everything at Busch Gardens is pristine!) The 17 story first drop is heart-pounding. Plentiful Gs! There are so many great coasters out there that even I had a hard time putting it here. A Bolliger and Mabillard classic!

6. The Riddler's Revenge - Six Flags Magic Mountain
Valencia, CA

This is the tallest, most inversioned, and fastest stand-up roller coaster in the world! Reaching speeds close to 65 mph, this Bolliger and Mabillard beauty will twist you, turn you, flip you,...you get the picture! You have to ride it to believe it!

5. Magnum XL 200 - Cedar Point
Sandusky, OH

One of the first mega drop stomach-in-your-throat
hypercoasters, the 205ft monster of a roller coaster is very
imposing from the ground! You can see Canada on a clear
day!! With drops of 194 and 157 feet, tight turns and
pretzels this Arrow designed roller coaster reaches speeds
up to 70 mph!

4. Kumba - Busch Gardens Tampa Bay
Tampa, Florida

Hopefully Bolliger and Mabillard will make more of this
type of 4-across sit down type of coaster. I had the chance
to ride this one after a huge downpour. (Yipee!) The cobra
rolls are powerful, the pacing is excellent, and the tunnel
near the end will make you put your hands down real
quick!

3.Raptor - Cedar Point
Sandusky, OH

A dive towards the concessions stand from a 119 foot 45
degree drop starts this wild ride! The 100 foot tall vertical
loop is only the start of many surprises. Corkscrews and
cobra rolls, a visually terrifying close encounter with the
ground, and the finale of a tight helix makes this one of the

best steel roller coasters in America!

2. Steel Force, Dorney Park
Allentown, PA

Built by D.H. Morgan Manufacturing, this colossal hyper-coaster towers above everything in the park! The first drop is a screamer! (205 feet!!) Steel force builds in some tricks along the way as well as an airtime filled bunny-hop finale!

1. Montu - Busch Gardens Tampa Bay
Tampa, Florida

Awesome! Incredible!! Great theming! After the first drop into the 'side-float-slide' (How Bollinger & Mabillard engineered that feat, I haven't a clue!), I was screaming, "NUMBER 1!! NUMBER 1!!!" and other incoherent babblings. I feel its much better than its brother up north, Alpengeist. The whole ride had me going, " WHOAA!! YIIKES!! ARRRGH!!" The adding of tunnels makes this ride unique also! If you don't ride any other coaster this year, make sure you get to this one!!!

Appendix B:

Ten Tips For Making Your Park Stay Most Enjoyable

1.Look for discounts before you go.

There are many places like supermarkets and fast food restaurants that have free coupons where you can save as much as 20% on the gate admission. If you don't live in the same town as the amusement park, call their city tourism branch and ask if any places in town have discount coupons. They will be more than happy to assist you! Take the time to search for these bargains before you go. It will be well worth it!

2.Remember where you parked your car!

Unless you have one of those cars that say 'OVER HERE, JOE!' it might be a good idea to be observant of the parking lot markers. They are usually posted on the light poles for easy reading. It's very embarrassing to search 30 minutes for what could have taken a second. Take the time to memorize your section code or write it down on a piece of paper. With thousands of people going to the park at one time, your vehicle can be easily lost in the shuffle. By the way, this has *never* happened to me. (Wink.Wink.)

3.Take sunblock, suntan or any 'Anti-Misery Stuff' along with you.

During the summer months, many parks around the country can reach temperatures near 95+ degrees! It's a good idea to use a high SPF sunblock to prevent yourself from looking like a roasted hot dog. Having some lip balm handy would be a good idea also. (Just don't share it with the whole planet. That's gross. Remember the "Saturday Night Live" skit?) If you're at the park at night, mosquito juice is a good thing to have in your personal care bag.

4.Drink plenty of water. *Drink water even if you are not thirsty.*

The sun has a way of zapping all the strength out of you and significantly decreasing your energy levels. Properly hydrating yourself (at least 1+ quart of water per hour in hot temperatures) prevents many instances of heat stroke and heat exhaustion which can occur.

5.Locate the First Aid Station & Lost and Found before running off anywhere.

This is another one of those things that only takes a minute to do. They are usually located near the entrance. Many a valuable article is taken to the lost and found by good and decent people. At the same time, limit the amount of expensive things you take inside!

6.Keep a budget of how much you will spend.

Food prices, parking, admission prices, ride tickets, souvenirs, games, ad infinitum! It all adds up to a lighter wallet at the end of the day. Keep tabs on your purchases so you won't be surprised coming home.

7.Wear broken-in shoes to the park.

You will walk approximately 5-10 miles while you are in the park. This is not the place to wear that new pair of dress shoes or high heeled shoes that you want to show off! (Remember, its an amusement park –not a Paris Fashion Show.)

8.Make sure you wait at least 45 minutes after eating to ride again.

Roller coasters and a full stomach don't mix! I have seen children coming off intense thrill rides and looking more green in the face than a turnip patch. Let your food digest! This is a great time to shop for souvenirs or try your hand at one of the many games in the park.

9.Don't Push Kids to Get on Thrill Rides and Roller Coasters!!

A lot of parents (especially fathers) like to drag their children on the latest 200 foot 5 G force pulling ride that comes along. If your son or daughter isn't keen on riding, don't force it. A scared kid on the ground is a terrified kid in the air! Let them grow into it.

10.Remember your purpose for coming.

Amusement parks and fairs are great places for families, friends, and loved ones to bond and have fun together. **Don't forget to bring a camera**! Cherish these moments. In a world of ever increasing complexity, simple times like these go a long way.

Notes

Notes

Notes

Notes

Notes

Notes